Midlife Business Ideas - Niche Websites:

How to Create and Monetize a Niche Website Through Affiliate Marketing, Advertising, and Information Products to Generate a Passive Income

The Midlife Business Ideas Series

The Midlife Business Idea Series is aimed at people between the ages of 30 – 50 that have always wanted to start a business and create freedom in their life. Building a business when you have responsibilities is very different from starting a business when you are care free in your early 20's. You can't afford to put everything you worked for at risk like your family, career and lifestyle.

That is exactly why the Midlife Business Idea series of books will focus on businesses that have 3 characteristics.

1. Easy To Start
2. Can be run part time
3. Create a passive income

The books are geared to be the start of your research process they are quick and easy to read or listen to (Get Audio version for free when you try a FREE Trial on Audible)
The information will help you clarify and decide if a business model is something you should pursue and how to get started.

Table of Contents

Introduction
Chapter 1: Why Niche Websites?
Chapter 2: Choosing Your Niche
Chapter 3: What You Need to Get Started
Chapter 4: Get Content for Your Website
Chapter 5: Affiliate Marketing
Chapter 6: Ad Revenue
Chapter 7: Information Products
Bonus Chapter: YouTube Traffic Source
Conclusion

Introduction

Congratulations on downloading *Midlife Business Ideas - Niche Websites: How to Create and Monetize a Niche Website Through Affiliate Marketing, Advertising, and Information Products to Generate a Passive Income* and thank you for doing so.

Many people think that starting an online business as a middle-aged person is too risky. Unfortunately, those people are wrong. Whether you are searching for financial freedom, looking for ways to finance your children's education or bolster your retirement savings, there is no better time to start an online business than now. As a matter of fact, starting an online business as a mid-lifer has considerable advantages. For starters, you have a wealth of professional knowledge to draw from that can help you as you start your business. You understand the value of having a good work ethic and the importance of time management. The best part of starting a business as a middle-aged person is that you understand how the middle-aged market thinks, which is a lucrative market to tap into if you want to create niche websites, but it is not the only market that you can appeal to when starting your niche website business, which is the topic of this book.

Niche websites are great ways to make money because they can help you create a passive income. Passive income is a powerful weapon to have at your disposal. Passive income is different from active income because, with active income, you are getting paid on a per hour basis. With passive income, you can make money from your initial time investment. If you build a portfolio of small niche website targeting different markets, you have the potential of always having a stable source of income. Mind you, building niche websites is not a get-rich-quick scheme. You need to put in work for this online strategy to work. However, if you do it the right way, there is a strong possibility that niche websites can offer you passive income and financial freedom for years to come. Due to the different ways you can monetize them, niche websites can form the foundation of a digital, location-independent business.

The benefits of niche websites are endless. Niche websites are relatively cheap to set up, and you can see a return on your investment relatively quickly. If you have no online marketing experience or even if you are an expert, the process of setting up a niche website is quite simple to do. Once you understand the process of creating a niche website, outsourcing or getting others to build niche websites for you is quite easy to do. Not only can you get others to build the niche websites for you, but you can also hire them at reasonable, if not, dirt-cheap rates. This ability to outsource the work of niche websites can help you build a portfolio of these quickly which diversifies and stabilizes your income. Another amazing benefit of niche website is the ability to earn money from different income streams, and you do not even have to sell your own products. You can just promote ads on your site or you can create different incomes streams from one site. The potential income possibilities from niche websites are limitless. All the different ways to take advantage of the highest advertising platforms and how to get traffic from search engines will be explored in this book.

Part one is all about laying the foundation of building a niche website and how to create one. In Chapter one, more attention will be given to why niche websites are great businesses to start and why you should start one will be explored. Chapter 2 will examine how to pick the topic of your niche website. In Chapter 3, the tools you need to get started building your niche website will be explained, and in Chapter 4, how to get content for your website will be discussed. Part two of the book is all about how to monetize your niche website. Chapters 5 and 6 will explain how to use affiliate marketing and ad revenue in order to monetize your websites.

Chapter 7 is all about how to create your own information products to sell, which will increase your earning exponentially, and a bonus chapter discussing how to use the power of YouTube to get traffic sources for your website will highlight one of the easiest ways you can help your niche website to succeed. Now is the time to learn how to make money from niche websites. Get ready to take notes. By the time you finish reading, you'll be readying to start your own site.

There are plenty of books on this subject on the market, so thanks again for choosing this one! Every effort was made to ensure it is full of as much useful information as possible. Please enjoy!

Chapter 1: Why Niche Websites?

Out of all the many ways to make money online, why should you start a niche website? Great question, and I'm glad you asked. This chapter will give you all the reasons why niche websites are the perfect way to start making money online. Before we get into why they are an ideal online business, we will first discuss what niche websites are in more detail.

There are often two categories of websites online. They are niche websites or authority websites. Niches are very targeted websites that focus on a specific topic. They are the opposite of authority websites. Niche websites have about twenty pages or less on the entire website. Some can even have one page, whereas, authority websites have a lot more content on them. Authority websites aim to be seen as a one-stop shop for a more general topic, compared to niche websites, that want to be seen as solving a specific problem or resource for a much smaller audience. Authority websites can take years to gain traction, but niche websites can gain traction a lot faster. For those who have a short attention span or want to find a way to make money online relatively quickly, niche websites are ideal. When you build a niche website, you are tapping into a billion dollar Internet advertising market. Online advertising accounts for a lot of money, so that means there are a lot of different ways you can succeed if you build a great niche website.

Now, for the more in-depth reasons why you need to set up a niche website. The first reason these websites are ideal online money makers is that they are really easy to set up. One does not have to be an online expert to create a niche website. There are lots of easy tools to use that can help you get your meet website up and running. These tools are so easy to use that you can even create a niche website after reading this book. (No worries, we will walk you through how to set up your niche website.) Niche websites also have an easy learning curve so you can pick up quite easily. Additionally, there are lots of resources that you can use to help build your niche website with this book being number one.

There are countless stories on the Internet of people who are making four, five, and six figures monthly from leveraging the power of a niche website. Some of these people are beginners themselves. There are lots of bloggers who utilize the power of niche websites, such as Alex Becker or Pat Flynn, who share their mistakes that you can learn from to help you succeed. Another great reason niche website work, and that is not often harped upon, is the ease of exit. Because they are so easy to set up, you can create one and move on to the next one if you lose interest in a topic. You do not have to be committed to the site long-term as if you were with an authority website. If you optimize the website correctly, you even have the benefit of building niche websites and moving to the next website as often as you would like.

Niche websites are also very cheap to start. You do not need thousands of dollars to get them up and running. You can get a website up and running for less than $20 a month. That's just foregoing a few cups of coffee of month or a week of lunches. In very extreme cases, you can even get your website up and going with no money, which we will discuss in Chapter 3. You also have to ability to utilize premium tools that can help your niche websites to go to the next level. This book will mention them, but we will focus on the free tools that are just as effective as the premium tools. Niche websites are easy to replicate, which means you can scale them fast. This is the second benefit of niche websites. Once you understand how to set them, you can follow the pattern to create different websites that target different audiences. The great thing about understanding the niche website creation process is that you can outsource them once you know how the process works which is the next reason why these websites are so great to start. You can always hire people to create your niche websites, do keyword research, create content, and even maintain your website to name a few tasks.

Most people use a more general method for outsourcing which includes hiring a few people or one person to do all the tasks. A better method to outsourcing is called micro-outsourcing. This means you hire one person who is really good at one task. So, instead of having one person to do everything for your niche website business, you have a team of people who all do what they are really good at which helps your niche websites to be of quality. So, for a person who is really busy, niche websites are the perfect way to supplement income in a hands-off manner while reaping the profits. There are also people who specialize in each website topic so you can easily find people who are comfortable and making these websites as long as you give them the instructions that you want. Popular sites to find remote workers include Fiverr.com, Freelancer.com, and iWriter.com, to name a few. There are thousands of sites that you can find reliable, cheap help from to help build your sites. Most people like to outsource virtual assistant help from the Philippines due to the cheap costs of acquiring one for your business.

One of the very most important reasons niche websites are ideal is that they serve as the foundation that can help you reach your financial goals. You can use a niche website to launch a different business or a different website. By creating a focused group of people that you can always market products to, niche websites can help you make money from years to come. If, for some reason, you do not want to work on your niche website anymore, you can simply sell it. They are the perfect exit strategies. Imagine creating a portfolio of ten to twenty websites that you can sell to other people for a big payday. Niche websites allow you that opportunity. And because they are so easy to create, you can create portfolio after portfolio with big payday after big payday easily and quickly as soon as you understand the process. As you set up your website, make sure you are installing Google Analytics so you can keep up with your site's metrics. Have great records of your niche website, including information like who is visiting your site, volume trends, and the amount of money you are making monthly can be the difference from having a mediocre or huge payday.

EmpireFlippers, Flippa, and FE International are just a few of the more popular places to sell your niche website. Sometimes, if your site is doing well, someone may ask you about buying the website from you. It is important that you know the number you want to sell your site for in case someone asks for it. When you begin making an income, niche websites often can sell ten to twenty times the monthly revenue that the site is bringing in. If your website makes more than $5,000 a year and you want to sell it, it is advisable that you use a website broker to help you facilitate the sale. For many, selling a site gives them the seed money to launch another business or to launch another business venture altogether.

As you can see, niche websites are the perfect opportunity to build a passive income especially if you are a person who is desiring financial freedom. You can easily create a portfolio of different websites and you have two strategies you can use when trying to set up your niche website. The first strategy is choosing a niche website topic based on your interest. This helps you enjoy the process of building the niche website better. The second strategy is to choose a niche website topic based on the profitability of the niche. You may not be as passionate about the project, but you are dedicated to building it based on the earning potential which can be just as inspiring. You also want to be sure that the topics you are discussing on your niche websites are evergreen, which means that the content can be consumed no matter what season it is. This way, you don't have to expose yourself to seasonal trends as you first begin. Once you get really good at building your niche websites, then you can focus on supplementing your evergreen websites with more seasonal ones. By building a portfolio of diversified niche websites, you can create different streams of income. Just like real estate, a diversified portfolio helps you to stay in good financial shape.

It is a no-brainer. Niche websites are the perfect way for you to start and create your online business. As a beginner, you will be able to pick up the skills rather quickly. If you make a mistake, you do not have to worry about being unable to recover from it. Niche websites are rather forgiving, and once you start creating them, they are rather easy to pick up on. If you follow the steps in this book, you'll be able to soon join the people who are making bookoo money from niche websites.

Chapter 2: Choosing Your Niche

The purpose of this chapter is to help you figure out which niche you should pick when starting to create your niche website. There are two main strategies you can choose from strictly: either creating a niche website based on your passion or creating a niche website based on profit potential. No matter what option you choose, a process can be followed to determine if a niche is a good topic to build a website around or not by looking at its profitability potential. It would be a shame for you to spend a lot of time building a website and then discover that you cannot make any money from it. This chapter hopes to prevent that pain and heartbreak for you.

If you are going to do the writing for your website yourself, it is advisable to start off writing about a topic that you are passionate about, but you have the option to decide if you want to be very focused about the topic or to be more general. For example, if you want to write in the baby niche, you have to determine if you just want to create a site about 'baby car seats' or make the niche sites about 'baby products' in general. Being super focused allows you to rank the site easily, but if your niche site is broader, you have more room to write about different topics so you do not get bored. You can decide what you want to write about, which is great!

If you are choosing a niche based on its profitability, you have to decide if you are going to outsource the writing or if you are still going to do the content writing yourself. If you have no idea where to begin when trying to pick a niche topic to write about, try this strategy. Grab a piece of paper and jot down five problems that people have, five things that people fear of, and five topics that you are passionate about. From that list, choose the top 10 things you are interested in writing about. If you need a little bit more help, you can consider looking into topics around the following niches:

- Making Money Online – Any topic in this niche is extremely valuable. Since there are lots of ways to make money online, this niche will not be difficult to find a topic to write about.

- Health – This niche encompasses so many topics. You can decide to try and tackle common or embarrassing illnesses like hemorrhoids or STDs. The possibilities are limitless!

- Teeth Whitening – This niche is evergreen because people always want to whiten their teeth. You can address different whitening techniques for chronic wine and coffee drinkers or the everyday joe!

- Yoga – This niche is popular amongst so many people. Whether they practice yoga for health reasons or spiritual reasons, you can find someone who is interested in learning more about yoga. There are also lots of yoga accessories in this niche, too.

- Drones – The popularity of drones is just beginning. This is the perfect time to get in on this niche and create a site for the beginner or enthusiast.

- Guns – People love their guns. This is a hot niche with lots of earning potential.

- How To Learn Something – Teaching new skills will never go out of style. This niche can help you make a lot of money from drawing upon your experiences, and you can even learn something new in the process, too.

- Dating – You can also help a lot of people with this kind of niche. With communication always changing, this niche can definitely provide solutions to people who have questions about this topic.

- Décor – There is no doubt that the décor niche is a very popular niche with many offshoots you can choose from. With many rooms that you can decorate in a house to different types of dwellings that you can decorate, there are plenty of topics you can choose in this niche.

- Weight Loss or Weight Gain – Weight loss and weight gain is an ill that plagues many people. This niche is guaranteed to help you make money, especially if you can help people lose weight the easy way, there is no way that you can't make money in this niche.

- Wedding – The wedding niche, no matter if you are targeting those who want a cheaper wedding or luxurious wedding, this is one niche in which you can't go wrong.

- Getting Pregnant – This is another great niche to target. There are lots of ways to approach this niche from the topics about sex techniques to get the sex of the child that you want to IVF options. This is one interesting niche for sure.

- Pets – Who doesn't love their pet, whether they are dogs, cats, or another type. This niche can focus on pet accessories or pet necessities to treating common illness. People love their pets and would love to spend money on their pets, too.

- Survival – This is a popular niche because many people are preparing for the world's end and becoming more sufficient. This niche is all about helping people to prepare, whether it is building underground shelters, learning how to grow their own food, or homesteading. This is an interesting niche that many more people are becoming interested daily.

- Beauty – There is no way that you can't make money with this niche. Whether you are targeting hair, makeup, skin, or clothes, the beauty niche always has trends you can discuss and money to be made.

- Nutrition – Nutrition is a popular niche because there are so many kinds of diets, and there are diets one can write about. Nutrition is very popular, and you can approach it from discussing foods, diets, kitchen gadgets, or even vitamins as starters, but the possibilities are really limitless.

- Baby– Who doesn't love writing about babies, and who doesn't love spending money on babies. The baby niche can be approached from many angles, from reviewing baby products to writing about the latest trends. This is a win-win niche for sure.

These are not every single niche you can write for. This is just a list to help get your wheels turning. One of the best things about niche websites is that you can write about any topic that you want to write about. Also, think about if you can write a hundred articles for this niche site or not. Remove any niches that you don't think you can write long-term for from the list. Once you have the list of topics you are interested in, it is now time to see if those topics will be profitable or not before deciding on your final topic.

Using Amazon is a great way to see how profitable a niche is. You simply go to Amazon.com and then look at the Amazon categories. Choose an interesting category and then look at the sub-categories. You want to look for products that cost over $100 and also have an above 3.5-star customer rating. You also want to see if the product has over ten customer reviews or not. If you are creating a niche that is a broader website, you'll want to make sure that the products you are perusing have accessories that can support it. This allows you to always create articles on your niche website that has links to other products that your readers can potentially buy. Along with accessories, also think of complementary products that go well with your niche that can help you create a complimentary niche in case you want to ever create another niche website. Amazon is a great way to see if there are profitable products for your website because the entire world uses Amazon. Another great place to look for products for your niche websites is on affiliate program websites like Commission Junction, JVZoo, or eJunkie. Make sure that you are making note of how much the commission for the products is. If you have quite a few products that you can potentially sell on your website, it may be a good niche. However, do not get discouraged if you do not see a lot of products because you can potentially create your own products you can sell which will help you make more money in the long run. Ideally, if your niche is one that people like to spend money on, you will be able to make money from the niche.

After narrowing your niche ideas down, you'll want to use Google to see next if people are searching for information related to your niche. Use the incognito search function so your web browsing history will not skew the results. Think of ten terms that someone will type in when they are searching to buy something from your niche. When you look at the search results that come up, what type of websites pop up on the first page? Are they forums or branded websites? Are they small websites or authority websites? If you have lots of small websites, forums, and Web 2.0 articles like Reddit or Squidoo, you may be able to rank for that site. Keep the list handy because we'll need it when trying to come up with content. If you see lots of big websites on the first page, you may need to look into another niche. Keep a list of your results to stay organized and focused until you come up with a winner. Here's how to think about this process. When you are looking for something to buy, what terms do you use when typing into the Google search box? Are you looking for reviews and testimonials or discounts and deals? A person searching for vacuums may not type in a specific word such as a 'name brand vacuum cleaner', unless they know that's what they want. Search terms they may use could be 'cheapest vacuum to buy' or 'replacement bags for a vacuum'. These types of words show an intent to buy. And you want to try to use search terms like that to see what results Google gives you when you search for them or topics that show people are intending to buy. Again, keep a list of your ideas because it will come in handy in Chapter 4 as we do more keyword research.

Once you have your niche and product ideas, you want to think next of ways to brand the website. Can you create a brand around the website? Can create a logo that promotes the site? Can you potentially sell the site to someone long-term? This will help you narrow down your niche topic even more. If you need help coming up with names for your website, you can use this resource: https://anadea.info/tools/online-business-name-generator. When you are thinking of a website name, try not to make it a direct search term that you may have found in your preliminary research. You do not want to name the website a keyword term because Google may overlook your site. Try to come up with a name that's related to your niche, but you can also brand it. For example, if we go back to the vacuum cleaner example, you do not want to use a specific vacuum cleaner as the website name. Perhaps VacuumBuyingGuide or VacuumPurchaseHelp will be better. You can let your creativity help you come up with a name that will show people who land on your site that you can help them with their problem. Branding is also important because you can potentially use any logos or tagline on merchandise, which we will discuss in Chapter

7 when we talk about creating informational products.

Narrowing down your niche can be a long process, but it is important to go through the research to make sure that the niche is profitable. It would not be fun to do all the work of setting up the site for your niche, but realizing that there are not any profitable products that you can sell. So, be sure to do your due diligence. Do not half-heartedly do this step. Once you have narrowed down your list of items, it is now time to think about setting up your site, which will be the topic of the next chapter.

Chapter 3: What You Need to Get Started

Now that you have your niche and domain name, it is time to set up your website. This site will help you go through the first steps you need to take to get your site up and running. We will go through how to purchase your website, what types of things to look for in a domain name registration and web hosting company, how to install WordPress, and the important pages that you must have on your website for peak performance.

The first thing you want to do is to purchase or register your domain name from sites like Namecheap, GoDaddy, or Bluehost. There are lots of sites for you to choose from. You can check out a few reviews if you'd like, but most companies do the same thing, so you don't have to spend too much time deciding which company to choose. Worst-case scenario, you can always move your domain name and web hosting company if you are not satisfied. As you decide which company to buy your domain name from, there are other things to consider when purchasing from a site.

One of the first things to think about when selecting a domain name company is their customer service policy. What options do they have to reach out to them if you have questions? Do they have chat or phone options? Which one of these is important to you? What are their operating hours? Do they have a lot of helpful resources? Do you see tutorials for people online or great customer reviews? After you figure out the answers to these questions, it is time to purchase your domain name.

Registering or purchasing your domain name allows you to own the website name. If possible, you will want to choose a '.com'. Most people view this type of website as legitimate once they visit, and it helps people to find your website easier. If there is not a domain name with the '.com' option available, other popular names include '.magazine,' '.info,' '.site,' '.review,' or '.co'. When you are checking for domain names, also be aware of the renewal charges. Every time you buy a domain name, you have to renew the domain name yearly. This renewal charge allows you to maintain ownership of the domain name. If you do not pay the renewal charge, you will no longer own the website. The renewal price will be listed, so make sure you can afford it. Sometimes, it is cheap to buy the domain name, but the renewal price can be a lot of money. You will also want to make sure the domain comes with some type of protection like 'Whoisguard', which protects your personal information. When you register your domain name without 'Whoisguard' protection when people look up the website, they can see your personal details that you have included in the purchase of the website, so you want to protect yourself if you can. Most companies include this type of protection for free, and you can renew it for a few bucks the following year when you renew your site.

After you purchase your domain name, you then need to buy a web hosting service. Web hosting allows your site to pop up in the browser when you buy the domain name. Web hosting is essentially the electricity that turns the light on in a domain's house. When selecting your web hosting options, try to purchase one that has the fastest loading times. This will ensure that your loading times are fast, and people will stay interested in the information on your site. Some hosting companies give you a free domain name once you purchase a web hosting package. Scout to make sure you get the best deal possible. You can often type in the name of the company you are interested in using and the word discount or coupon to see what types of deals appear in the search engine results. They often cater to first-time customers, and you can definitely secure a deal if you do a quick Google search.

After selecting your web hosting package, the next step is to download a content management system. For the purpose of this book, we will advise you to use WordPress, which is a very popular and easy-to-use platform that allows you to create your website easily and quickly. With your hosting package, you have the option to install WordPress with just a click. Most hosting companies have a tutorial about how to do it, which is extremely easy to do.

The great thing about WordPress is that it allows you to build your website from scratch or a theme template can be used. The theme template allows your website to look professionally designed and to optimize the website for purchases. Popular themes include Focus Blog theme, AuthorityAvon, or MyThemeShop, to name a few. Some themes are free while some are paid; there are also premium themes. Depending on your budget, you can decide which will be the best option for you. WordPress has lots of great free and premium themes, so paid themes are not necessarily a better option. It is all up to how you optimize your theme that determines if you make money, not how pretty the theme looks. There are pretty sites that do not make money and ugly sites that make a lot of money. Where you place ads and how you utilize the theme is more important than your theme's aesthetic. So, do not spend too much time on your theme. Make one and start creating content and driving it to your site so you can see what content begins to make the most money for you.

After you have selected your thing, it's time to add your plug-ins to the site. A plug-in is a piece of software that helps you optimize the theme. Some are free to add, while some may cost a fee. Again, your budget will help you figure out which plug-ins are the best ones to use. Here are few to get you started:

- TablePress – This helps you to create pretty tables that allow you to compare and contrast features of your website.

- Floating Social Bar – This plug-in easily helps others share your info to social media. It is easy to use and thankfully keeps your site moving fast.

- Outbound Link Manager – This helps you manage your outbound links. These are the links on your website that go to another place. They can be a 'nofollow' link or a 'dofollow' link. To rank for SEO, you want to mostly use 'dofollow' links for a webpage. However, you would enter a small code for the 'nofollow' link so the page you are linking info to will not receive any of your ranking juice for the keyword. This plug-in helps you to make your affiliate links as 'nofollow' so Amazon or the sites you are selling from receive any juice from your SEO efforts.

- Pinterest Pin It Button Image Hover and Post – This helps people to share your images to Pinterest. To make it more effective, you can include a call to action.

- Free Tools to Grow Your Email List, Social Sharing, and Analytics by SumoMe – This is a well-rounded plug-in to have on your site because it helps with your site's growth. You can see what content your visitors are interacting with the most. You can also use it to help build email lists.

- Social Locker – This is a great plug-in to use because it requires readers do a social action like share a tweet or post a content that's locked behind the action. It is extremely helpful when trying to spread your info across social media.

- Click to Tweet – This is another great plug-in to use as it makes your information great to tweet. It also looks professional and helps spread links to your site across social media if people use it.

- Q2W3 Fixed Widget – This plug-in helps your sidebar widget stay in place so they can see the side bar as they scroll down below the fold. This is extremely helpful because it helps people to always see your side content and even more helpful if you recommended products in your sidebar.

- EasyAzon – This helps you get the affiliate links you need from Amazon easily. Instead of having to sign into Amazon, this plugin connects to Amazon which helps you link to affiliate products a lot faster.

- Akismet – This plug-in helps prevent spam from taking over your site. It stays up-to-date with the latest spam tricks and is a good site to use.

- Jetpack by WordPress.com – This is a great plug-in to use to boost your site's overall effectiveness.

- Yoast SEO – This helps your SEO on your site so you can rank for keywords easier. The higher you can rank for keywords, the more money your site can bring in.

- W3 Total Cache – This helps your site load faster. A faster loading time means more money for you.

- WordPress Backup to Dropbox – This plug-in is important to have because it backs up your WordPress site to Dropbox in case your site ever gets hacked or go down. You will be protected.

- Contact Form 7 – This is a custom way to create a 'Contact' page that's easy to use and looks extremely professional.

- Google Analytics – This plug-in helps you keep track of people who are visiting your site and what they are looking at. This is important to have because it is a great way to measure your efforts.

- Google XML – This helps Google bots to scroll your page easier so you can appear in the SERPs or search engine results pages.

- AWeber or MailChimp – Choose one plug-oin so you can connect your autoresponder to your website. This plug-in allows you to capture emails from people to build your email list so you can continuously market to them.

- Multi Plugin Installer – This helps you install all your plug-ins at one time which helps you save time.

This makes your niche website look even more professional. If you know any artistic people in your family or friends with kids, they may design the logo for you for free. You can design the logo yourself by using a free stock image and the Canva site which gives you logo templates to choose from. A logo can always be redesigned, so get an adequate logo and keep going to the next steps.

Once you have these added, next is to install a few pages. The pages you want to have are as follows:

- About Us – This page explains what the niche site is all about and how it can help them. It also gives little info about the site's founder.

- Privacy Policy – This lets the site's visitors know how you are going to use their info. You can create a free one by going to freeprivacypolicy.com.

- Contact Us – This page is important because it legitimizes yourself and gives people lots of different ways to contact you. Include a physical address that can be a virtual office, a phone number that can be a free Google Voice number, an email address, and a contact form. There's nothing more frustrating than trying to reach someone and not having any way to contact them.

- FTC Affiliate Disclaimer: There are lots of free templates you can use. This is important so people will know that you may receive a commission from the products that you create. This builds trust with the readers so they know that you are honest and open about the information on your site.

This chapter has walked you through the basics of setting up your niche website from buying your domain name and web hosting package as well as how to install your WordPress system. Once you install WordPress, you will want to install helpful plug-ins to make your site run smoothly and pages that will legitimize your website. While it's exciting to determine what the logo and name of the site are going to be, you don't want to let indecision prevent you from moving forward with building your website. Think carefully and select what you would like, but do not agonize over the decision. The most important thing is to start so you can learn quickly and make adjustments fast. Now that your basic website is set up, it is time to add content to your niche website, which will be discussed in the chapter.

Chapter 4: Get Content for Your Website

Doing keyword research is important because it is the way to tell if people would be interested in your website or not. A keyword is simply the word used when someone is searching for something in Google. A site tries to rank for a keyword, so when someone types that keyword into Google, their website comes up. Ideally, when ranking for a keyword, you want to become the first stop that pops up on Google. However, if you can be on the first page, that's helpful. Keyword research is the process of choosing words to rank for that will allow you to be on the first page on Google. Selecting the right keywords will help more people find your site which means more money for you in the long run. Essentially good keywords can make or break your site, so it is important to find keywords that can help sustain your site.

There two types of keywords: long tail keywords and short tail keywords. A short tail keyword is something that's really broad like 'healthy diet' or 'kitchen appliances'. These are really difficult to try and rank for, but a long tail keyword contains at least three words and is highly specific to a solution your target audience is trying to solve. For example, a long tail keyword would be 'best vacuum for hardwood floors'. It is easier to rank for long-tail keywords because people who are entering these keywords are looking for solutions. This is important to do because you can be passionate about a topic, but if people are not searching for the topic, then you are not going to make money. This step allows you to really see if your niche can make money or not. We will want to use the Google Keyword Planner for this process and the Google search box itself. Paid tools you can use are Market Samurai and Long Tail Pro. For the beginner, focus more on understanding the process and then you can decide if you want to invest in pricy tools or not. We will now take some of the keywords that we used in our preliminary research to come up with a topic by using the free Google Keyword Planner Tool.

This is a free tool to use if you have a Gmail account. To access the tool, type in Google Keyword Planner, and then sign in. This a free tool to use so you do not have to pay for anything, although, Google may give you the impression that you have to order a campaign. Google wants you to buy something from them so the opening page can be a little aggressive, but there is a way to get around it. To get over the prompts when you sign in, follow these steps.

1. When you sign in, Google may ask a few questions about your main advertising goals, but click on the small letters in blue that say 'Experience with Google Ads?' so you can skip this step.

2. Then, you will go to a page that asks about your campaign type. Select 'Create an account without a campaign' in blue under those boxes.

3. Then, confirm your business info. This will take you to the main page.

4. In the top right corner, you should see your Gmail account info, but look to the left and select the Tools option. The very first panel on the left will be labeled 'Planning'.

5. Under 'Planning', there is the Keyword Planner. Select the 'Keyword Planner'. You may have to select the 'Explore account' option first, which will then allow you to access the Keyword Planner.

6. Once you select the Keyword Planner option, you will then have the option to select two options: 'Find keywords' and 'Get search volume and forecasts'.

7. You'll want to select the 'Find New keywords' option and make sure the US is selected as the target country. Using the filters, set your keyword volume between 800 to 5,000. This means the amount of people that search for that term monthly. This number will help you find keywords to rank for that are not that competitive but still can help you rank on Google.

8. Enter your search terms from the preliminary research you did in Chapter 2. You can enter multiple keywords or one at a time. Also, try to find keywords that utilize question words such as how, what, why, etc. This will also help you create the content on your website. We're aiming for twenty keywords that we can use when creating content for our niche website.

Here are a few other search criteria you can use to help you find keywords to use on your website:

- Intent To Buy - Using your ideas from Chapter 2, search for more keywords in the keyword tool that suggests the purchase. Words can be 'discount,' 'coupon', 'reviews,' 'best,' or 'quality'. Again, the easiest way is to think about what keywords you would type in before you buy something or if you are looking to purchase something.

- Cost Per Click - When you are entering keywords, a price shows up beside it. This price is what advertisers pay Google when someone types in that word and clicks on their ad. If the price is high, it shows that people are willing to pay big bucks for the keyword which signals it is a lucrative market.

- Trends – This is another important thing to consider when choosing your keyword. Is the niche you want to create the site about a seasonal niche that happens only on certain holidays or is it an evergreen niche which means it can be sold all year long? It is good to have a combination of seasonal and evergreen niches when you are more established, but starting out, you may want to focus on evergreen niches.

- The Monthly Search Volume - When doing keyword research, try to find a keyword that has a volume from 800 to 5,000 monthly searches and try to rank for the keyword. Now, this number may vary for some people. Some people want to look for keywords that are over 1,000 up to 20,000 searches a month. As you get better with ranking your sites, you can choose this number for yourself; however, staring with 500 to 1,000 monthly searches can help you rank faster and more easily than a higher volume number.

Once you have your twenty keywords, it is time to write the content! (I hope you are getting excited. This is the fun part.) Every article you write should have about one to two to keywords. We'll start off with ten articles, and then you can write more articles that you can drip later. Dripping the content you write is when you write all your content up front for your website or at least ten articles, and then schedule one post a week after that to stay up-to-date. WordPress is powerful because it gives you this option. Looking at your keywords, try to come up with ten articles you can write or you can even hire someone to write. The articles should contain a few requirements:

1. They are valuable and unique. Using keywords can help your site rank, but nothing helps your site rank faster than proving great content. The point of the niche website is to provide helpful content to others so be sure that your site is doing just that.

2. Using media-rich content such as infographics, videos, and pictures can also help your articles rank for the keywords you want. Do not be afraid to use Canva to create content for your website. Just remember that if you are linking to other videos, these videos should not push your customer to buy something from them. That will take away from your sales, so be careful when you are linking others' videos content. Creating your own content with YouTube will be discussed in the bonus chapter.

3. The articles are at least 500 to 2,000 words. A sweet spot to aim for is 1,500 words. The longer your articles are, the more Google likes them. Remember, don't stuff your website with keywords. Try to make them look natural and use one to two keywords per article.

4. Have a table of contents on your website that points readers to specific places on your site. This shows Google that your site is well-organized and a great resource to readers.

5. If you are writing the articles yourself, you can do article spinning. This is when you write one article and put it in an

article spinner software and let it create a new content for you. If you use this method, be sure to double-check your content. Also, if you want to just outsource the writing, Fiverr.com, upworke.com, and iWriter are great places to start looking.

6. If at any point, you need to write reviews about products that you haven't personally bought, here are some tips. You can read the user's manual, which is very helpful, and read the product description. You can also read the reviews of people who bought the product themselves and pay special attention to the 1, 3, and 5-star reviews. You can also search for other reviews of the product itself.

Other popular topics that are great to write include frequently asked questions and answers to questions that you see people post about the product in other forums. Any content that will answer potential questions that people may have about a product or even help them make a purchasing decision is the content that you want to have on your niche website.

If you want to hire others to write for you, here are a few questions that you will want to ask the writers before you hire them. You ideally want to target writes who are native English speakers that live in the US or Canada. You also want to offer them about $1 for 100 words. Provide an outline for the article that you want them to write so you have an idea of how they respond. Then, give them a deadline and let them complete the assignment. Once they finish, you can decide if you want to continue with them on long-term projects or not.

Once you have your articles written, you then want to optimize your on-site SEO. SEO stands for search engine optimization. This step makes sure that your keywords are in optimal places that will help you get on the first page of Google. You do not want to write your keywords in a way that isn't natural, but keep it as natural as possible, or use the keywords in your writing in a way that it makes sense. However, you do want to put your keywords in three key places. The first place to put your keyword is in your URL. WordPress allows you to modify the posts' URL, so include your keyword in the URL. The next place you want the keyword to appear is in the meta-description. When you search for something in Google, the information under the website that pops up is called the meta-description. You can use the Yoast SEO Plugin to edit your meta-description to your website. The last place you want to put your keyword in is the title of your articles. It is easy to get caught up in all the rules of SEO, but the most important thing to remember is that you should be providing value to your readers and offering great content. If you are doing that, you should be fine.

After optimizing your on-site SEO, the next place you want to optimize is your off-site SEO. The most important way to do that is with backlinks. Backlinks are a link from another website to your niche website on inter-links between posts on your website. You use your keyword as anchor text, and then link it to another article on your website. Backlinks serve as co-signs. It lets Google know that your niche website is quality and trustworthy. Building backlinks is a slow and steady process. The easiest way to get started is to link your articles to each other so people can use your website as a resource. You should also link to your homepage as well. Then, you can set time aside to link to other authority websites that show you are proving content. You can also leave your article's link in related articles in the comment section. Slowly building your backlinks is an important way to show your site's quality, and it is also a major factor if you should ever sell your site. The good think about backlinking is that you can outsource it as well.

While SEO is important, another important way to maximize the visitors that come to your site is by having an email list. You should offer a freebie that will entice them to give you their email—more on that in Chapter 7. If people give you their email, you can always market to them. Popular email autoresponders include AWeber and MailChimp. AWeber is free for the first two weeks, and MailChimp is free up to your first 2,000 subscribers. Both of them have their respective plugins that you can use on your website as well.

Choosing keywords are an important part of the niche website creation process. It is important that you select ones that you can rank for and create valuable content around those keywords. You can find keywords using the Google Planner Tool or even using the Google autosuggestion box. Once you have your keywords selected, create valuable content that uses one or two keywords in the article and optimize the keywords for SEO in the article and by creating backlinks. Now that we have addressed creating unique and valuable content, (by writing them yourself or using someone else to write it), it's time to figure out how to monetize your content or make money from your content, which will be the subject of the next chapter.

Chapter 5: Affiliate Marketing

When you have a niche website, there are few different ways for you to make money from them. Starting out, people often don't have products to promote, so they promote other people's products. Affiliate marketing is perfect for the beginning niche site creator due to its ease of use and ability to let you sell products faster without having to pay anyone to create a product for you. Affiliate marketing can also be beneficial if you form relationships with certain program creators as they have their own reward system built in their affiliate program. You just have to find the right platform for you. Affiliate marketing is an important aspect of niche site creation, and it is the subject of this chapter.

To begin affiliate marketing, you simply sign up for an affiliate marketing website, browse their products, and choose to promote products related to your niche. Once you sign up, you will be given an affiliate link, and then you put that link on your website in your written articles. Any time someone clicks on the link and purchases the product through your link, you will get a commission. If you don't have any products, affiliate marketing is a great way to begin monetizing your site. There are lots of different affiliate websites you can choose from to promote your product.

When you are looking for an affiliate website to promote, there are a few things you must consider

- The first thing is to look at the product itself. Is the advertising copy on the product well-written? Are the graphics used to promote the product nice-looking? Would you purchase the product? Looking at how professional the product looks will help you see if you are going to make sales or not. If someone clicks on the link on your site to go to an unprofessional page, that may prevent them from purchasing, which means a loss sale for you. Thus, make sure that the website and graphics of the product look professional so you can have a conversion.

- The next thing to consider when choosing an affiliate program is when the payments are going to be made and how the payments are disbursed? Some commission payments are made weekly, bi-monthly, or monthly. Some are even paid out every 60 or 90 days. Before signing up with a commission website, it is good to know how often payments are going to be made so you can budget accordingly. Not only is the payment schedule important, but also how you can receive the funds. Will the payments be made via PayPal or deposited into your checking account automatically? Does the affiliate program charge any fees for disbursing payments on certain platforms? This information is good to know because fees can eat up your profits.

- Another important to know how refunds are handled. This will help you understand how they can affect your affiliate paycheck. You also want to make sure that having a lot of refunds will not negatively affect your paycheck. On the other hand, you want to make sure that they have some sort of protection against people who can game the system, so it will adversely affect your site as well.

- How does the commission structure work? Sometimes, commissions can be low until you sell so many products, at which point, the commission will go up. Other commission structures revert back to the low commission rate every month and do not let you benefit from the higher commission rate monthly.

Know how the commission rate works so you can make the most amount of money possible.

- How the affiliate program handles their cookie tracking is another piece of vital information to know. Cookies are the small tracking software attached to your affiliate link when you sign up for an affiliate program. If someone lands on your niche site and clicks on the affiliate link without making a purchase, will you still get paid if they visit at another time? Will you still get paid if they click on someone else's link to purchase even if you were the first person whose link they clicked on? Knowing how long the cookies tracking lasts is important to make sure that you are getting credit for pushing someone to the affiliate site and not anyone else.

- You will also want to see if you get paid once off by the product you are promoting or if there are multiple payments you will get paid from if you send a customer through someone's funnel. This can help you choose a very profitable product to promote.

- The last factor to consider is how fast it takes you to get approved for the website. Sometimes, it takes a while for you to get approved as an affiliate website; sometimes, it's instant. Some affiliates also require that you have certain requirements before they approve you, so it is good to know this information before signing up for an affiliate website.

Since you now know what types of questions to look at when selecting an affiliate website, let's look at different affiliate marketing techniques that you can use.

One of the most popular strategies with affiliate marketing is to review lucrative products. Your reviews will help people make a purchasing decision, and as a result, you will receive a hefty commission for your insight. Ideally, you want to market products at least $100. Some people have more success with even higher-priced products. There is no hard or fast rule, but the higher-priced items seem to be a better way to start out. Once you have more experience, you can take on lower-priced items if you are more comfortable. Again, focus on setting up the site and learning the process so you can become a pro at what type of products work best in your niche.

A popular place to find expensive products is to use Amazon or Wal-Mart websites once you are approved to be their affiliates. These two sites are some of the most popular websites and have built-in trust already, so people will be more likely to trust your reviews. The great thing about Amazon marketing is if someone clicks on your link and they do not buy the product, you can still commission on whatever products they purchase. This is extremely helpful during the holiday season.

To get started with Amazon or Wal-Mart, just sign up for an affiliate website on their respective websites. Once you become an affiliate, you will be able to select different links and pictures to promote on your website. Using these two platforms to promote lucrative websites or any product is one of the most popular and most effective ways to make money with affiliate marketing. Since the commissions are lower compared to some other affiliate programs, some marketers prefer to use other affiliate programs. However, the built-in trust from Amazon and Wal-Mart can help you have a higher conversion rate and possibly balance out the negatives. It just depends on your niche website. Other popular websites to find products to promote include Share-A-Sale, Click Bank, Commission Junction, eJunkie, and JVZoo. These sites have their own sign-up process. You can peruse their products that determine what you want to promote. You also have the flexibility to sign up for multiple affiliate networks for your different niches.

The next affiliate marketing strategy is to promote books after you do a review on them using Amazon Kindle e-books. Similar to the previous strategy, this focuses on promoting books solely. It is extremely effective if you want to create a book website. Amazon Kindle has countless genres you can choose from so you can always find a book you are interested in promoting. This strategy can be taken to the next level by promoting your own e-books depending on the niche. Creating your own information products will be discussed in Chapter 7. Amazon is a popular place to use when promoting books. There are other e-book sites that also have affiliate programs, like SmashWords or Kindle. Don't be afraid to mix and match the affiliate links on your website.

The next affiliate marketing strategy to consider is called launch jacking. This strategy involves creating a niche website around a product that has not been released yet. This will help people learn more about the product, and your site will be seen as an important resource for those who are interested in learning more about the new product. Even if the product is not released yet, you can create a pre-order affiliate link that will let you reap the benefits from purchases that people make from the link. If you create testimonials and reviews or predictions about products, people are likelier to trust you and buy from you. Also, people who tend to be first-adopters are avid fans, and you can always create content for them since they love the products that would be promoted on your website. Thus, try to get their emails so you can always market to them and have a steady stream of income. Excited, obsessed readers are great customers to have!

The next two strategies are for those with limited money who cannot afford hosting or buying a domain name but still want to create an affiliate site. This method is a great starting place, but it is advised at some point to have ownership of your own niche website by purchasing the domain name. If the website was to ever go down using this strategy, you would lose all your content since you do not own the website. Protect yourself and your business by owning your own property. However, you have to start someplace, and this is a good technique to use. The first strategy uses Squidoo pages to create a niche website. They put their links on the Squidoo pages and then promote their products that way. This is a good way to make money from Amazon as well. For people who do not want to buy a website, you can just create a website to promote Amazon products and make money as well. The second strategy involves using YouTube.

Instead of a niche website, you create a niche YouTube website that allows you to promote content around the niche and promote products in the videos and in the description box. If you do not want to put your face on camera, you can easily do voiceover videos, whiteboard videos, or animation videos with a site like GoAnimate. If you have extra funds, you can even hire someone to make a video for you using Fiverr.com. The bonus chapter will address more ways to use YouTube to drive traffic to your site in more detail.

Affiliate marketing is great because it isn't a hard sell. Customers can look at the info on your site and then decide if they want to buy from the link or not. Hence, make sure that you are writing helpful, convincing content that can help people make the decision to buy once they click on your links. The best thing about affiliate marketing is that there is a wealth of products to choose from, so you are guaranteed to find something that you can promote. Once you figure out what website you like the best, you can choose to promote their products only. Or you can promote different products from a bevy of affiliate marketing site. The more you work with sites, you'll figure out which affiliate marketers you like to work with. You will also begin to figure out what type of content converts best with the information you are trying to sell since each niche has different buying practices. The key to figuring all this out is to practice, practice, practice building your niche websites.

When scouting potential affiliate markets to use, make sure that you have your questions answered. Also, figure out which affiliate strategy you want to use. Do you want to promote one product all throughout your niche site or one product only? Do you want to promote books or music or software? Whatever you decide, sign up to the affiliate marketing site of your choice. Then, sign in to your affiliate dashboards and put your links in your article. It's advisable to do reviews of products that you know personally. Otherwise, you can still write reviews as long as you research the reviews of others. However, if you don't want to deal with affiliate marketing, there is another way you can make money online, and that is to buy using ad revenue to monetize your sites, which will be the topic of the next chapter.

Chapter 6: Ad Revenue

Using ads to monetize your website will be the topic of this chapter. This method of monetization is similar to monetizing with affiliate marketing in that you have to have great content that people want to read. When you monetize with ads, you do not make money based upon if people buy products or not. This method of monetization can be a lot easier because you do not have to sell anything. However, if you are going to take advantage of using ads to monetize your strategy, you often have to have some type of traffic flowing into your site. This traffic signals to advertisers that your site is worth advertising on. Even if you do not have a lot of traffic just yet, some advertisers are still willing to work with you. If ad revenue is your selected revenue model, there are different ad revenues that you have to decide to use as advertisements on your website. You can choose from CPC, CTA, CPM, or ad revenue models.

- CPC means cost per click. Another name for this model is PPC or pay-per-click. Just as the name says, you get paid based on if people click on your ad or not.

- Similar to this model is CPM or cost per million or how much it costs per thousand impressions.

- CPA, the last revenue model, means cost per action, wherein you get paid dependent upon if the people who click on the add take a certain action or not. It could be responding to the ad with an email or phone number. It just depends, though.

Your chosen revenue model depends on how many visitors you get to your website. Similar to signing up for an affiliate management program, you also have to sign up for an ad revenue program. Here are the questions you should consider before signing up to a website:

- Can you get paid the way you want to get paid?

- What's the minimum threshold they pay out? Some sites wait until you accumulate a certain amount of money before paying you.

- Do you have a process or certain amount of traffic to qualify to use the ad service?

- Are the reported reports in real-time? Knowing how they measure their results is an important factor for you to know.

- Are you required to only use their ads or do they allow you to use other ads?

- Do they have support that can help you figure out the best place to put your advertisements so you can maximize profits?

These are a few preliminary questions that can help you select the ad network to be used. Next, we suggest a few ad networks for you to check out.

The first ad network is Google AdSense. This is definitely one of the most popular ad networks that people signed up to use. There is an approval process, and you can choose from the type of revenue model you will use. To make the approval process easier, try to have quality content on your site already and avoid using any other type of ad networking. You'll also want to have Google Analytics already on your site. If you installed the plug-in from Chapter 3, you should be fine.

Great ad networks for beginners to check out are Propeller Ad Network and Bidvertiser. Once your site gets older and gets a stable level of traffic, you may want to look into Chitika and Adbluff. Hilltop Ads is another great ad network for sites with more traffic. A middle-of-the-road solution for beginner and more experienced niche creators would be Media.net.

Worst-case scenario, if you are not approved by any website, you can reach out to related businesses and see if they would be interested in advertising on your website. You can give them your rates on a one-sheet. A one-sheet lets business know all about your niche website and why they should advertise with you. It should contain a few things; lots of information can be found when you log-in to your Google Analytics website with your Gmail account email:

- Goal – What is the purpose of the one-sheet? What is your goal in creating one? Make sure that you have that clearly highlighted so people who read it will not be confused.

- An engaging title – This should address a problem that your site can help people solve who will be advertising on your site. Make sure that this is easy to understand so they will not be discouraged from working with you even though you are small.

- Demographics of people who are visiting your sites – This should show information including the age, sex, ethnicity, income, hobbies, and background of people who are visiting your site. You should also include how they are visiting your website and the types of devices are they using.

- Your volume – Be sure to include how many people are visiting your site monthly and daily. If you can even include the times, that would be great.

- Testimonials and positive comments – If anyone has left a nice comment about your site, include it so future advertisers know that your site has an impact.

Any other information that will convince them to advertise with you should also be included. Ultimately, you determine how much your advertising rates should be, so make sure the price you asked is backed up by the value your site offers which should be included in the ad sheet.

In the long run, making money with your ads is all about experimenting. Sometimes, ads convert better depending on the color and the location they are on your site, so it is important to test, test, and test. It may take some work, but it is definitely worth it. In the next chapter, we will be discussing one of the best ways to monetize your site is through making information product.

Chapter 7: Information Products

Information products are digital products related to your created niche. Creating your own information products is one of the most lucrative ways to make money online. You do not have to worry about being approved by anyone. You create the products and sell them on your site. Moreover, you do not have to worry about dealing with shipping or customer service since most do not have a refund policy. Information products require some work up front, but once you create them, they can bring in income in the years to come. They are also great because you can put them on affiliate websites so others can sell the info product for you. Therefore, you would benefit by selling them directly and getting paid when people sell the product for you. This chapter will be dedicated to helping you create your own information products that you can link to your website.

The easiest products to begin creating are e-books. An e-book can be a simple PDF document that you link to your website, addressing common issues surrounding your niche. These are great because once you create them, you can continue to sell them. You can also put them on Amazon as an additional income source. If the e-book is the digital file, you can create an e-book's audio file which would be considered an audiobook. Audiobooks are extremely lucrative in the market, and they are growing every day. Offering both the e-book and audiobook as a custom package is a way to boost your profits from your niche website. You can also submit audiobook or e-books to an affiliate website so other people can sell the products for you, maximizing your profit even more. Writing e-books are a lot easier to do than people can imagine. If you create an outline for the book, you can dictate the book so you do not have to type it out. Then, give the dictation file to a transcriber so they can edit it for you. You can make the process as easy or as hard as you would like, but the main point is to get an awesome e-book written either by yourself or someone else. Similar to e-books, templates that will help solve readers' problems are also easy to create and to sell at a premium price. Templates are a lot simpler and faster to create, but just as valuable.

Another popular digital product to create is a video course. A video course utilizes videos to educate readers about a topic related to your niche. They can be considered premium products. Video has a built-in expectation that it is more valuable than a book. So, you can earn more money by offering content in video form. If you create a PowerPoint or some type of guide to go along with your video course, then the course becomes a multi-media course, allowing you to increase the prize even more. You can use YouTube private videos or Vimeo to film the course and then give the links to people who buy the courses. You can edit them by using simple editing software that comes on your computer. Similar to video courses, you can also create seminars. A seminar would just be a speech or talk that you record. This type of content is also valuable because people can listen to it while they're doing everyday activities. You also have the potential to repackage seminar audio content as a podcast.

Creating t-shirts with a print-on-demand website is another easy way for you to monetize your website. You can create a t-shirt around your brand by uploading a graphic to TeeSpring or another print-on-demand site and directing your customers to that link. Then, TeeSpring will take care of fulfilling the order for you while you pocket the profits. T-shirts are not the only items that a print-on-demand site offers so you can choose from lots of products that you can promote on your site. While TeeSpring is one of the most popular print-on-demand websites, there are a lot more others including Amazon, PrintAura, Printful, and Zazzle. Print on demand is such an awesome option because you do not have to worry about fulfilling any orders. The print-on-demand website takes care of that. Once you figure out what types of designs work for your niche, you can hire a graphic designer to create the designs for you, which will allow you to scale this side of your business faster. For the more adventurous person, you can use Canva to make your own graphics. Since Canva already has built-in templates, you can tweak the templates and upload them to the print-on-demand websites yourself.

You can also offer your services or web-based software as another way to monetize your site. If you have a service business related to your niche, you can use your website as a traffic source to your business. Make sure your rates are set so you can reap a profit worthy of your time with the services you are going to offer. Consulting, coaching, accounting, or any other skill that can be sold can be offered to boost the income from your niche. Try to create different packages or different levels so people can choose what they would like to pay for. Web-based software is another extremely lucrative income stream to add to your niche website because you can set it up as a recurring payment, which means you can get paid month to month on it. You can hire someone to make such software for you or create it yourself using a DIY software or an app builder. This allows you to create a multitude of different products that you can link on your website. Creating your own products is a definite win-win situation and one that is highly advisable.

When deciding how to create these informational products, you can decide to create these products yourself or you can outsource the work so you do not have to worry about it. Popular apps or sites to find freelancers would be Upwork.com, Fiverr.com, or even Freelancer.com. Once your products are created, you can play around with the price point. You can choose to price your books at $27, $99, or $149, or any price that you want—totally up to you. When you are selling your products, do not sell yourself short for you may realize that people are willing to pay a lot more than what you think they will pay.

After you decide the price, you then have to figure out how people can buy it from your site. If you are using WordPress, you can either direct people to a website such as Big Cartel which is connected to your website. This method allows you to let another site take care of the security settings. Variations of this method could include using JVZoo to create a button on your website or putting a PayPal button or using eJunkie. If you do not want your info hosted on another site, you decide to use a plug-in like WooCommerce and transform your site into a shop. Make sure that your website is protected security-wise, which means putting a security plug-in on your WordPress site that protects customer's credit card info as well as getting an SSL certificate. It is doable, but a lot more work is involved.

So, there you have it! Here are all the ways that you can create different products on your website. You have e-books, templates, audiobooks, video courses, seminars, print-on-demand products, software, and apps. After you decide what you are going to sell, you can determine if you will sell on your WordPress site yourself or direct them to another website to buy the product. The great thing about informational products is that once you create them, you can always get other people to also sell them for you, so the product can work double-time making money for you. Informational products are also great offers to people in exchange for giving them your email. The next chapter is going to focus on using YouTube, an often underused resource when combined with niche websites, as a traffic source to get more people to your site.

Bonus Chapter: YouTube Traffic Source

YouTube is a powerful tool you can use to drive traffic to your niche website. The great thing about YouTube videos is that it can help increase traffic to your website, which means more sales and more profits for you. The chapter will highlight the ways you can leverage YouTube to get more views for your niche website. Most people do not take advantage of this awesome resource because they think you need to have a lot of views to use it, but you do not need a lot of views to make a lot of money. Just 1,000 extra visits to your website is enough to make more money if you have your site optimized.

Just like using a niche website, the way for this YouTube strategy to work is to have quality content on your YouTube page. People will not watch your videos if it is not addressing their problems. So, make sure that the videos you create are high-quality and addressing the concerns related to your niche. Aim to make about ten videos initially and then you can organize them in a playlist. This playlist is effective because once people watch one video, they may become addicted and watch more than one, boosting views for your YouTube page and your website.

Similar to when you write your articles for your website, you also want to optimize your videos for SEO. If you need to look up more keywords using the Google Keyword Planner Tool, you can. Another easy way to figure out what keywords to use is to take advantage of Google's suggestion box. When you are trying to rank for a keyword, you want to use Google. Google the keyword and see if a video appears in the search results when you Google it. If not, that's the keyword you want to use in your video, so your video can pop up when people Google it. People love videos, so using videos is an optimal way to direct people to your website. Once you have your keywords, it is important to optimize the keywords on the video itself. How?

- The first way to optimize your video is to use keywords in your title. You want to make the title informative, but also helpful. Try to use the keyword naturally in the video to avoid being penalized by Google.

- The next place to optimize for keywords is in the description box. Take advantage of the description box and write long descriptions. However, divide it into smaller paragraphs. You also want to have a link that is easily accessible to people above the fold that they can click on without having to extend the full description box. You can play around with the description to figure out what type of description you prefer, but do not be afraid to write upwards to 200 to 300 words. Remember to add https:// before your link so it can become a clickable link. This step is important because people are lazy. If they cannot click on the link, they will not take the time to copy and paste the link and put it in the search bar. They just won't.

- Tags are the next place that you want to optimize your keywords. Try to use about ten to twelve tags per video-related keywords.

- Also, take advantage of optimizing your thumbnail with an eye-catching thumbnail and you can use a main keyword in the description there as well.

When you actually create the video, you want to optimize the content in three important ways. First is to take advantage of overlays in the video. You can create overlays directing people to your call to action which is the second way to optimize your video content. At the end of every video, give the viewer an instruction to do. You can use your overlay to direct them back to your site with the link included. Tell people what to do, so they can do it. Additionally, when you create your website, encourage people to subscribe and like your channel. That way, you have a built-in list that you can continue to market to.

Remember, when you set up your YouTube channel, don't forget setting up your 'About' page. This helps people to learn more about you and know where to find you on all social media platforms. This helps people form a relationship with you on all your platforms. Also, do not be afraid to interact in the comments. People love interacting with YouTube creators. To really take your YouTube strategy to another level, you can partner with other YouTubers in your niche. You guys can do videos together and share audiences. It is a definite win-win, but make sure you make it as easy as possible for the person you want to connect it.

Do not overlook the power of YouTube to grow your niche website. It is a great way to drive traffic to your site and bolster your asking price when you finally sell your niche website. Most people do not take advantage of using YouTube. Do not be like those people. Just a few views can help you make more sales and increase your bottom line. When you sign up for YouTube, make sure that you optimize your page and have a well filled out 'About' page so people can find you outside of your YouTube channel. If nothing else, having a YouTube connected to your niche website can increase your asking price if you were to ever sell the niche website one day. Do not leave that money on the table. Happy YouTubing!

Conclusion

Thanks for making it through to the end of *Midlife Business Ideas - Niche Websites: How to Create and Monetize a Niche Website Through Affiliate Marketing, Advertising, and Information Products to Generate a Passive Income*. Let's hope it was informative and able to provide you with all of the tools you need to achieve your goals whatever they may be.

Niche websites are an excellent way to start an online business. Thanks to their low start-up cost, high ROI, and ease of creation, they can help the beginning online marketer start making money relatively easily. Niche websites are smaller websites focused around a tightly-defined topic. Niche websites are often under twenty pages, and some are even one-page. Using keywords, niche websites try to rank on the first page of Google so people can find the website and buy products through the website. If a person has a system of creating niche websites and ranking them, their earning potential is unlimited.

This book goes through everything a person needs to know to start their own niche website business. In the first chapter, we discussed the reasons why niche websites are the ultimate foundation to beginning an online business.

The strategy for choosing your niche was discussed in Chapter 2, and in Chapter 3, how to start your niche website was explained. Chapter 4 walked you through the process of creating content for your site, and Chapters 5 and 6 explained how to monetize the site through affiliate marketing and ad revenue respectively. Chapter 7 gave attention to the best way to ways creating your own information products to watch your profits skyrocket. And the bonus chapter discussed how to leverage YouTube to drive more visitors to your site, which surprisingly many people do not use. Using the information in this book will help you start your niche website so you can start earning income passively.

No matter what your ultimate financial goal is, you want to begin creating a niche website to create a passive income. The more you create them, the easier the process becomes. The easier it becomes, the more websites you can create and the more diverse your online portfolio can become. Thankfully, niche websites give you the option to make money passively years to come or to sell them for a big payday. The choice is yours. It is time to get started.

Finally, if you found this book useful in any way, a review on Amazon is always appreciated!

Visit: https://midlifebusinessideas.com/books/ for more books

Kindle Publishing:
How to Create a Passive Income with a Kindle Publishing Business

Midlife Financial Intelligence:
Proven Business And Investment Strategies to Create Passive Income

Midlife Investing Strategies: A Comprehensive Guide to Investing in Your 40s